THE BOA CONSTRICTOR

BY
WILLIAM R. SANFORD
CARL R. GREEN

EDITED BY
DR. HOWARD SCHROEDER
Professor in Reading and Language Arts
Dept. of Elementary Education
Mankato State University

PRODUCED AND DESIGNED BY
BAKER STREET PRODUCTIONS
Mankato, MN

CRESTWOOD HOUSE
Mankato, Minnesota

ROCKINGHAM COUNTY PUBLIC LIBRARY

OUTREACH
MADISON
MAYODAN

EDEN
REIDSVILLE
STONEVILLE

J597.96
S

LIBRARY OF CONGRESS CATALOGING IN PUBLICATION DATA

Green, Carl R.
 The boa constrictor.

(Wildlife, habits & habitat)
 SUMMARY: Describes the physical characteristics, habits, and natural environment of the large, non-poisonous, snake that suffocates its prey by squeezing it very tightly.
 1. Boa constrictor--Juvenile literature. (1. Boa constrictors. 2. Snakes.) I. Sanford, William R. (William Reynolds). II. Title. III. Series.
QL666.C63G74   1986   597.96   86-32868
ISBN 0-89686-320-4

International Standard Book Number:
Library Binding 0-89686-320-4

Library of Congress Catalog Card Number:
86-32868

ILLUSTRATION CREDITS:

Cover Photo: Cris Crowley/Tom Stack & Associates
David M. Dennis/Tom Stack & Associates: 5, 6, 26, 28, 37, 42
Bob Williams: 9, 18
John Cancalosi/Tom Stack & Associates: 10, 20
Marty Cordano/DRK Photo: 11
Phil & Loretta Hermann: 12
Robert C. Simpson/Tom Stack & Associates: 15
Cristopher Crowley/Tom Stack & Associates: 17, 38, 41
John C. Murphy/Tom Stack & Associates: 24-25
Tom Stack/Tom Stack & Associates: 31
Brian Parker/Tom Stack & Associates: 32, 45
D. Cavagnaro/DRK Photo: 35

Copyright© 1987 by CRESTWOOD HOUSE, Inc. All rights reserved. No part of this book may be reproduced in any form without written permission from the publisher, except for brief passages included in a review. Printed in the United States of America.

Hwy. 66 South, Box 3427
Mankato, MN 56002-3427

TABLE OF CONTENTS

Introduction 4
Chapter I: Snakes that squeeze their prey 8
   A warm-climate snake
   A family of colorful giants
   A tough and useful skin
   How boas "hear," see and smell
   A strong and agile body
   Slow and silent movement
Chapter II: The problem of being cold blooded ...21
   A boa's diet is meat and more meat
   Feeding takes a long time
   Seventy-five percent water
   Even boa constrictors have enemies
   A solitary animal
Chapter III: Birth of the young 29
   Survival isn't easy
   Molting gives the boa a new skin
   Hunting for larger game
   The cycle repeats itself
Chapter IV: Myths about boas 35
   People learn their fear of snakes
   Boas are useful, dead or alive
   Where can you see a boa
Chapter V: Boas don't need much attention 43
   Handling a boa
   What do the experts say
Map 46
Index/Glossary 47

INTRODUCTION:

Janet liked Mexico from the moment she stepped off the airplane. After the cold winter in Ohio, the warm spring air of Mazatlan felt wonderful. And her Mexican "family" spoke good English. Being an exchange student was going to be fun!

Señor Paz drove along the beach so Janet could see the Pacific Ocean for the first time. Señora Paz was talking about their plans for the week. Janet sat in the back and chatted with her new "sister" Marta. She wondered if Marta would like Ohio when it was her turn to visit Janet's family.

"Mama," Marta said suddenly, "Janet must meet Hector, don't you think? Poor Hector needs a girlfriend."

Marta's parents laughed loudly. "Yes, of course," Señor Paz said. "I'm sure Janet will like Hector as much as we do."

"Who's Hector?" Janet asked.

"Oh, he lives with us," Marta explained. "He's very slender and he has lovely dark eyes." The car pulled up at the Paz's house before Janet could ask any more questions.

After Janet unpacked, Marta took her outside. "Hector's a little shy," Marta said. "He's hiding under the house."

Janet saw that the house was built high up off the ground.

"Mazatlan is very hot in the summer," Marta explained. "This type of house lets cooling breezes blow the heat away. It's also a good hiding place for rats—but Hector keeps them away."

Marta led the way. As Janet's eyes adjusted to the dim light under the house, she looked around. "Where's Hector?" she asked.

Something was moving in a dark corner. A long, slender shape was wriggling toward them. Janet jumped back, ready to run.

This is what Janet saw moving toward her—a boa constrictor.

"It's okay," Marta laughed. "That's Hector!"

Janet didn't know whether to laugh or cry. Hector was a giant snake! Was he about to attack?

Marta saw the fear in Janet's face. "Don't be afraid," she said. "Hector is part of the family. Besides, we're too big for him to eat. He only eats rats and other small animals."

Jane could see Hector clearly now. She guessed that he was at least ten feet (3 m) long. His skin was a golden tan with dark brown diamonds. The snake's forked

Janet guessed that Hector was about ten feet (3 m) long.

tongue flicked in and out as it moved slowly toward the two girls.

"What kind of snake is he?" Janet wondered.

Marta reached down and Hector coiled around her arm. "Hector is a boa constrictor," she said. "We found him when he was still tiny. He crawled out of a bunch of bananas at the city market."

Janet stroked Hector's back. His scales felt dry and smooth. "Doesn't he miss the jungle?" she asked.

"Hector has a good life here," Marta said. "Sometimes he crawls into the house to take a nap. But he never chews the furniture or makes a mess. My aunt doesn't like him, though. She almost fainted when she sat on the couch—and there was Hector, sleeping under the cushions!"

Janet looked into Hector's lidless black eyes. What would her friends in Ohio think? She couldn't wait to tell them all about the boa constrictor named Hector.

CHAPTER ONE:

Snakes are members of the reptile family. Other typical reptiles are lizards, alligators, and turtles. Like their reptile cousins, snakes are scaly, air-breathing reptiles. Most lay eggs, but a few give birth to live young.

Unlike the mammals, reptiles are "cold-blooded." This means that they can't control their body temperature. Leave a snake out in the blazing desert sun, and its blood will boil! In a similar way, ice crystals form in a snake's blood during freezing weather. In both cases, the snake will die.

Snakes such as the boa constrictor have been around for thousands of years. They evolved from lizards that lived in burrows and tunnels. In place of legs, they developed long, flexible bodies that slid easily through narrow openings. At the same time, the snakes lost their eyelids and their hearing.

Snakes that squeeze their prey

Boa constrictors belong to a family of snakes called the *Boidae*. This family includes the three largest snakes on earth—the anacondas, the pythons, and the boas. Herpetologists (experts who study reptiles) consider the *Boidae* to be rather primitive. That's because they still have small hip bones. The hip bones are hidden inside the snake's body, but you can see a boa's rear legs! Each tiny "leg" is covered by a horny claw. The males

The boa has rear legs that are covered by a horny claw.

use these claws to stroke the female during mating.

Unlike rattlesnakes and cobras, the *Boidae* are not poisonous. These great snakes kill by coiling their bodies around their prey. Despite what many people think, boa constrictors don't crush their victims. Instead, they simply squeeze so tightly that the animal can't breathe. Death comes from suffocation.

Boa constrictors don't crush their victims. They slowly suffocate them.

A warm-climate snake

The boa constrictor's scientific name is *Constrictor constrictor*. It is one of about thirty varieties of boas that live in the Americas. Other boas are found in Asia, North Africa, Madagascar, and the Pacific islands. In the Americas, boa constrictors range from Argentina to northern Mexico. A three-hour's drive from the southern border of the United States will take you into boa constrictor country in Mexico.

Only the rubber boa *(Charina bottae)* is found in the

The rubber boa is the only boa found in the United States.

Emerald tree boas are found in tropical South America, where they spend much of their time in trees.

United States. This small, eighteen-inch (46 cm) boa lives in pine forests of the western states. It is a silver-green color and feeds mostly on small rodents. Rubber boas spend much of their time burrowing in the ground.

Another interesting boa is the emerald tree boa *(Boa canina)*. Bright green with white markings, these boas live in tropical South America. They spend much of their time in the trees, where they feed on birds and squirrels. When an emerald boa curls around a tree limb, it looks like a bunch of green bananas.

A third boa is the Cuban boa *(Epicrates angulifer)*. Cuban boas are found only on Cuba and the Isle of Pines. These ten-foot (3 m) boas are yellow-brown with dark diamond markings. Because Cuban boas prey on bats, they hunt mostly at night. They find their prey with sensing organs that detect the body heat of other animals. Boa constrictors lack the Cuban boa's heat detectors.

Large or small, boa constrictors have adapted to a variety of habitats. Most boas are found in tropical rain forests, but others live in grasslands and in near-desert areas. Boas are seldom found in highland country, and none live above the three thousand foot (914 m) level.

A family of colorful giants

The boa constrictor is truly a giant among snakes. Some Central American boa constrictors grow to fourteen feet (4.1 m), and weigh eighty pounds (36.5 kg). The largest boa ever captured was 18.5 feet (5.5 m) long. Even the largest boa constrictors cannot compare with the anacondas, however. A South American anaconda can grow to twenty-nine feet (8.7 m). Stretched out, an anaconda is equal in length to five tall people! However, the *Constrictor constrictor* averages eleven feet (3.3 m) in length.

A boa constrictor's skin is beautifully colored and marked. Most have dark brown diamonds and spots on a golden tan base. The markings often take on a reddish color near the tail. Boas found in Mexico and Central America tend to be less colorful.

A tough and useful skin

The boa constrictor's skin is well adapted to its way of life. The outer skin is made of tough keratin. Human fingernails are made from a similar material. Touch a boa, and you'll know at once that the skin is neither wet nor slimy. A snake's skin is dry and smooth to the touch.

A boa's skin is dry and smooth.

Although snakes have scales, they're not like the scales of a fish. You can scrape off a fish's scales, but not a snake's. The boa's scales are really folded parts of the skin. The scales overlap, with the edges pointing to the rear of the snake's body. That design allows the snake to glide smoothly across rough ground. The belly scales, in fact, grip the ground and help push the snake forward.

After months of rubbing on rocks and tree limbs, the boa's skin becomes worn and ragged. The boa solves that problem by shedding its old skin. The process is known as molting. As the old skin peels away, a fresh new skin waits underneath. Boas molt more often in warmer climates than they do in cooler regions.

How boas "hear," see and smell

The boa constrictor senses the world in a different way than other animals do. For one thing, boas don't have ears in the usual sense. They "hear" by picking up vibrations from the ground with their bodies. Even quiet footsteps cause the earth to tremble ever so slightly. That signal alerts a waiting boa constrictor to danger—or the chance for a tasty meal.

Like most snakes, boas can't see as well as humans do. They're good at spotting motion, but they can't focus sharply. Also, the lack of eyelids means they can't shut their eyes. In bright light, the pupil closes down to a narrow slit. Having their eyes on the side of the head presents another problem. Each eye sees a somewhat different view. Lacking binocular vision, boas can't judge distances very well.

The boa does not have eyelids. In bright light, its pupils close to a narrow slit.

To make up for these handicaps, boa constrictors have an excellent sense of smell. Their nostrils pick up scents from the air just as other animals do. Even more sensitive is Jacobson's organ, a taste-smell sense in the roof of the mouth. When a boa's tongue flicks out, it gathers tiny particles from the air and ground. The tongue then carries the particles back to Jacobson's organ. The information collected in this way helps the boa track its prey, find a mate, or avoid danger.

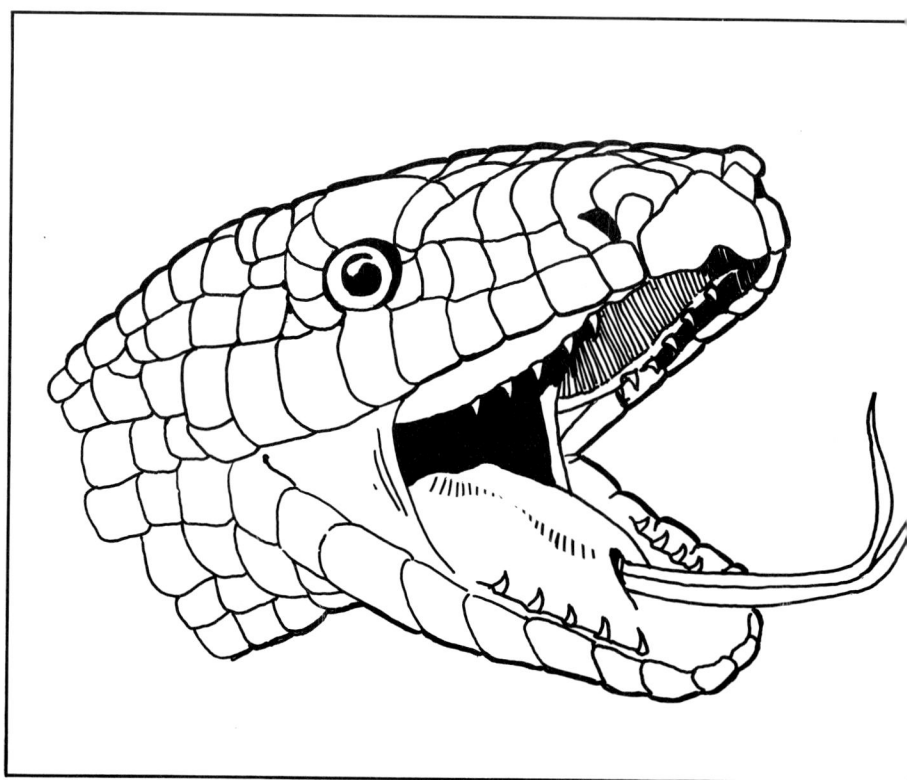

The Jacobson's organ helps the snake taste-smell the world around it.

A strong and agile body

From head to tail, the boa constrictor's body is well suited to its way of life. Inside the slender head, its mouth is lined with needle-sharp teeth. The teeth slant backward to help the boa hold its prey. The harder a rat struggles, the deeper the teeth sink in. The teeth aren't used for chewing, however. After the rat is dead, the boa's jaws swing open to allow it to swallow the animal whole.

Behind the head, a snake's organs are laid out in a long line. The kidneys, for example, lay one behind the other. The liver is long and narrow. Boas have two lungs, but the left lung is much larger than the other. The stomach stretches to hold and digest animals much larger around than the snake itself.

Herpetologists compare the boa's skeleton to a strong chain. The "chain" is made up of several hundred bones called vertebrae. A special joint locks each vertebra to another and allows a movement of only twenty-five degrees. Despite this, the large number of joints gives the boa constrictor great flexibility.

Slow and silent movement

A moving boa constrictor seems to glide across the ground without effort. The boa's stomach muscles move its belly scales back and forth in waves. The scales push against the ground and propel the snake forward. The boa also can curve its body to get a better grip on a smooth surface. In cartoons, snakes move in a series of humps, but a real boa's body hugs the ground.

Because snakes move so smoothly, people think they're fast. That's not true. Boa constrictors can move rapidly only for a short distance. They tire quickly because their blood doesn't carry enough oxygen. If a boa is traveling any distance, it glides along at only one mile (1.6 km) an hour. The boa constrictor also swims well. Its long left lung keeps it afloat, and the snake can go for a long time without breathing.

Most people will see boa constrictors only in a zoo's reptile house. The snakes adapt well to captivity, but their lives are very different in the wild. To see these beautiful snakes at their best, one should study them in their natural habitat.

As with most wildlife, it is best to study boas in their natural habitat. This is a Cook's tree boa.

CHAPTER TWO:

The boa constrictor has adapted to many different habitats. Most boas live in tropical jungles, where they spend much of their life in the trees. Temperatures as high as 110 degrees F. (50 degrees C.) don't seem to bother them, as long as they can find some shade. In drier, scrub brush habitats, the boa lives in burrows. People also find them in swamps, sugarcane fields, and near their farms.

The problem of being cold-blooded

Like all reptiles, the boa constrictor is cold-blooded. That doesn't mean that it has icy cold blood. Cold-blooded means that a boa can't keep its body temperature constant. If the weather turns cold, the boa must warm up or die. Generally, it has three choices: it can generate heat by moving around, it can find a warm burrow, or it can lie in the sun.

A sunbathing boa soon faces a new problem. The snake can't stay in the hot sun too long. Since it doesn't have sweat glands to cool the skin, it must find shade when its body temperature rises. Living in cold climates would create an even bigger problem. A boa's large body warms up slowly, and a cold boa would be too sluggish to go hunting.

A boa's diet is meat and more meat

Boa constrictors are meat eaters. They prefer live prey. Studies of their kills show that they hunt lizards, chickens and other birds, opossums, mongooses, rats and other rodents, dogs, and porcupines. Large boas also have been known to catch small deer and ocelots. As long as the prey weighs less than fifty pounds (23 kg), a good-sized boa probably can swallow it.

Like the other giant snakes, a boa constrictor often lies in wait for its prey. Its colors blend with the leaves and grasses. When a large, unwary lizard runs by, the boa strikes. Sharp teeth hold the animal as the snake coils around it. The lizard fights for breath, but the boa's grip grows tighter and tighter. In a few minutes, the struggle is over.

Boa constrictors don't always wait for their prey to come to them. They may climb trees to catch birds, or crawl into burrows to kill a rabbit. Despite all the stories that people tell, boas don't crush the bones of their victims. Sometimes they do push and pull the prey into a shape that's easier to swallow.

Feeding takes a long time

After the kill, the boa constrictor must work the lizard into its mouth. With its double-hinged jaw stretched wide, it swallows the prey head first. Little by little, muscles in the boa's throat and body push the lizard back to the stomach. A flood of saliva coats the prey and eases the task. Because snakes don't chew their food, all digestion takes place in the stomach. Strong stomach juices will dissolve almost every part of the lizard.

But digestion is a slow process. A small lizard may disappear completely in a few days. A rabbit, however, could take two weeks. Larger animals can be seen as bulging lumps in the boa's middle for even longer. Cool weather slows down digestion. When the process is over, only feathers, hair, quills, or claws remain. The boa expels them as waste.

A small lizard will keep a boa going for several days. After eating a large animal, the snake will not feed again for many weeks. This feeding pattern makes it possible for boas to survive for long periods without eating. A well-fed snake, in fact, will ignore a prey animal that walks in front of its nose. In a Paris zoo, a boa once lived four years without eating. The snake drank water, but refused all the food that was offered.

This boa constrictor recently ate a large mammal and will probably not eat again for several weeks.

Seventy-five percent water

The boa constrictor's body contains more water than most other animals. A full-grown boa is about seventy-five percent water, compared to a human's sixty-six percent. A boa's diet supplies much of the water it needs, but it also drinks from pools and streams. When drinking, the boa puts its head into the water. Throat

Like all boas, the body of this South Pacific island boa is about seventy-five percent water.

26

muscles pump the water into its body. When it's thirsty, a boa will drink for two or three minutes without stopping.

Since boas don't sweat, they retain water better than mammals do. In addition, they lose very little moisture from their lungs when they breathe. This system allows a boa to go for weeks without drinking. If a boa loses too much water, however, it will die. A loss of ten percent of its body weight can be fatal.

Even boa constrictors have enemies

Every wild animal has its natural enemies. The boa constrictor is no exception. Large snakes, wild pigs, hawks, mongooses, badgers, and other carnivores prey on young boas. As the boa grows longer, its list of enemies grows shorter. Only alligators, panthers, and ocelots present much of a threat to a ten-foot (3 m) boa constrictor.

Much smaller enemies known as parasites are also dangerous to the boa. Mites and ticks, for example, live in the folds of skin between the scales of most boas. Herpetologists believe that these parasites cause the bad temper of the Central American boas. Most wild snakes also play host to worms and one-celled parasites called protozoa. These invaders live in the snake's muscles, liver, stomach, and lungs. As long as the boa stays healthy, the parasites don't seem to cause much harm.

A solitary animal

For all of its size and strength, a boa constrictor is not an aggressive animal. The Hollywood movies that show boas dropping out of trees onto innocent natives are wildly inaccurate. Indeed, boas are slow moving, solitary creatures. They do most of their hunting at night.

You could walk through boa constrictor country for many days and never see one. Skilled herpetologists know how to find them, however. They've put together a good picture of the Central American boa's life cycle.

Even brightly-colored boas, such as this South American rainbow boa, can be difficult to find in its natural habitat.

CHAPTER THREE:

The Central American jungle lies warm and damp under a clear January sky. Birds sing and monkeys swing through the tall trees. On the jungle floor, a large male boa constrictor catches the scent of a female boa. Normally he would ignore her. But this is the mating season.

The male catches up with the larger female. Their courtship begins as the male flicks his tongue rapidly and crawls over the female. He raises his claws and rubs them against the female's body. The claws make a loud scratching noise. Finally, the male wraps his tail around the female and the two-hour mating begins.

Birth of the young

The female will carry her young for five to ten months. The length of gestation depends upon the temperature. Hot weather will shorten the period. Unlike the egg-laying snakes, boas and anacondas give birth to live young. As the months pass, the female continues her solitary life. The male has gone off on his own. As the time of birth draws near, the female finds a suitable nest in a hollow log.

In July, the female gives birth to about forty young boas. The usual range is from twenty to sixty. The smallest newborn boa is fourteen inches long and the longest is twenty-five inches (35 to 62 cm). The average newborn weighs only two ounces (57 grams). Soon after the last boa is born, the female leaves the nest, never to return. The newborn are on their own.

Life is dangerous for young boas, and many die in the first few weeks. Three are eaten by an anaconda, and several others are caught by hawks. One young male is lucky. He finds shelter and a hunting ground well supplied with mice. In eighteen months, he grows to thirty-five inches (87 cm) and fourteen ounces (397 grams). During these months, he catches and eats fifty-five mice.

Survival isn't easy

The young boa survives by hiding from danger. His colorful skin blends in well with the leafy jungle around him. He seems to know that he's too slow to run from an enemy. One day a mongoose finds him in the open. The boa tries a bluff. He raises his head and makes a loud hissing noise. Then he pretends to strike, just as

Large boas have very few enemies.

if he has poisonous fangs. The mongoose circles the boa, unsure of itself. The boa shakes his tail, making a rattling noise in the dry leaves. That's too much for the mongoose. It goes off to find easier prey.

As the boa grows larger, fewer enemies see him as a possible meal. He begins to hunt larger game. One night he catches a large tree rat. The meal keeps him satisfied for several weeks. He's now three years old, and over five feet (1.5 m) long.

31

Molting gives the boa a new skin

The boa is restless. He hasn't hunted or eaten for several weeks. His skin is torn and ragged, and it is losing its bright colors. Thousands of ticks pester him. The shields over his eyes are clouded. He can't see very well, and he spends most of his time in hiding.

Finally, the molt begins. The boa first loosens the skin around his lips by rubbing against a rock. Then, as he wriggles forward, the old skin peels back. It looks a little like someone pulling off a dirty sock. This time, the old skin comes off in one piece. The last time he shed, the skin around his tail hung on for several days. The new skin is brightly colored, and the new eye shields are clear.

After molting, this Haitian boa's skin is bright and shiny.

Like many other snakes, the boa seeks out a pool of water after molting. He plunges in and seems to enjoy his swim. Perhaps the molt causes a loss of moisture which must be replaced. One thing is certain. The boa will soon pick up a new cargo of parasites.

Hunting for larger game

At five years of age, the boa is almost fully grown. He now stretches twelve feet (3.7 m) from nose to tail. He spends a lot of time coiled lazily around a tree branch. Today, the boa is hungry. When evening comes, he slips down to the ground. His tongue carries the scent of a wild pig to the Jacobson's organ.

The twenty-pound (9 kg) pig is drinking at a water hole. The boa seems to know that he can't sneak up on this fast and agile prey. Instead, he waits beside the path to the water hole. In a little while, the pig comes trotting by.

The boa strikes as the pig goes past. His teeth dig deeply into the animal's neck. The pig kicks and squeals, but its struggles only drive the teeth deeper. The boa coils around his prey. Now the pig is caught in a strong band of muscle. It bites at the snake, but its teeth slide off the scaly skin. The pig's squeals grow weaker as it fights for breath. Just minutes after the boa struck, the pig gasps and dies.

Swallowing an entire pig takes several hours. When the boa is finished, his middle bulges hugely. Slowly, he drags himself off to a hiding place. Digesting the pig will take many weeks. He won't be hungry again for a long time.

The cycle repeats itself

The jungle doesn't change much during the winter. Even without falling leaves and cold weather, instinct tells the boa constrictor that it's the mating season. He crawls restlessly through the jungle, looking for a female.

A week passes, and still the boa continues his search. On the tenth day, he picks up an exciting scent. When he catches up with the female, she seems to be waiting for him. He hisses and flicks his tongue at her. The courtship is underway.

Months later, the female gives birth to thirty tiny boas. At this time the male is miles away, coiled up in his favorite tree. He doesn't see the farmer who stumbles on the nest. The farmer once saw his favorite dog killed by a boa, so he doesn't hesitate. He kills the newborn snakes with his machete. He doesn't know that hundreds of years ago his ancestors worshipped the boa.

CHAPTER FOUR:

Giant snakes have been worshipped for thousands of years. In the Americas, both the Maya and Aztec Indians carved huge boas from stone. One of the Aztec's most important gods, for example, was Quetzalcoatl. They believed that this god came to earth to teach them to grow corn. Quetzalcoatl's statues show him as a "feathered serpent"—half bird and half snake.

Myths about boas

Snake worship has almost disappeared from the world. Even so, people still tell tales about giant snakes.

There are many myths about boas, probably because most boas are so large.

Here's a little test on boa constrictors, based on the myths that people tell about them. Which ones are true?
1. Boas are poisonous two months of the year.
2. Never flee from a boa. The snake can crawl faster than you can run.
3. Boas sneak into unguarded cattle pens, where they suck milk from the udders of the cows.
4. In time of danger, a female boa will swallow its young. When the danger is past, she spits them up again.
5. Large boas kill and swallow people every year.
6. A boa must wrap its tail around a tree or rock before it can squeeze its victim to death.
7. A boa can knock you out with a butt of its head.
8. Even Hulk Hogan would lose a wrestling match with a full-grown boa constrictor.

As you probably guessed, all of the statements are false. Most of the myths go completely against what herpetologists have learned about boas. From where do such stories come? Some have a small basis in fact. When it's in danger, for example, a boa may spit up a recent meal. If it has eaten some small snakes, the half-digested food may seem to contain the boa's own young.

Other myths are based on the fact that boas **are** strong. But a butt from its head can't hurt you. Being butted by a boa would be like having a five-year-old child run into you. As for wrestling with a boa, a strong man or woman can win the match. The trick is to take a firm grip on the snake's neck just below the head—and don't let go!

People learn their fear of snakes

Many of the myths about boa constrictors grow out of fear. Are people born with their fear of snakes?

People are not born with a fear of snakes.

Experts say that this emerald tree boa would not scare little children, and that adults learn to be afraid of snakes.

Harold and Mary Jones set up an experiment to find out. They showed a six-foot (2.4 m) boa constrictor to people of all ages. Children under the age of two didn't show any fear. The two- to four-year olds were cautious without being frightened. After the age of four, the children started showing real signs of fear. Adults were the most fearful of all.

The Jones' decided that people aren't born with an instinctive fear of snakes. They learn their fears, probably by watching parents and other adults.

Boas are useful, dead or alive

People may fear boa constrictors, but they also put them to use. In parts of tropical America, for example, the mongoose was once imported to catch rats. In a short time, the mongoose population exploded. The animals began to prey on chickens, ducks, and other valuable birds. The farmers brought in boa constrictors to control the mongoose population.

In a similar way, other Latin Americans use boas to control mice and rats. That works well as long as there aren't any small farmyard animals around. The boa will eat a small dog as quickly as it will a big rat.

Even though the meat is edible, few people hunt boa constrictors for food. Instead, they hunt the big snakes for their skins. The skin is tough, flexible, and waterproof. Properly treated, a twelve-foot (3.7 m) skin can be stretched to twenty feet (6 m). Leather workers turn the skins into costly wallets, handbags, and boots.

Some people object to the trade in these skins. They believe that killing snakes upsets the balance of nature. Many governments agree, and the trade in snakeskins has been greatly reduced.

Where can you see a boa?

A zoo in Philadelphia showed Americans their first boa in 1875. After that start, other zoos added boa constrictors to their collection. The snakes adapted quickly to captivity. In the wild, they probably live no more than ten or twelve years. A captive boa, however, lived twenty-three years at an English zoo.

Seeing a boa constrictor at the zoo may not excite you. The giant snakes seldom put on a show. They lie in tangled heaps, inactive and half asleep. Well fed and content, they ignore the crowds pressed against the glass.

Another way to learn about boa constrictors is to visit a natural history museum. Museums set up displays that show the snakes in their natural habitat. You can see a boa coiled around an ocelot, or study a female as she gives birth. One thing is certain. You'll be impressed

An emerald tree boa shows off its markings.

by the great size of these giant snakes. Twelve feet (3.7 m) of snake takes your breath away!

There's one more way to see a boa constrictor up close. You may have a neighbor who keeps a boa as a pet!

Boa constrictors can make good pets, but experts don't think it's a good idea to make pets of any wild animal.

CHAPTER FIVE:

Most people who want a pet choose a dog or a cat. Others set up a fish tank or buy a singing canary. Very few want an exotic pet such as a monkey or a lion.

Hardly anyone thinks of keeping a snake. People who do keep boa constrictors, though, say they make excellent pets. They can be found in pet stores, where a three-foot (91 cm) boa sells for about $100 (US).

Boas don't need much attention

People who own boa constrictors enjoy their exotic pets. For one thing, boas are quiet. They never bark or scratch the furniture. They don't have to be taken for a walk. If their owner is busy one day and forgets to feed them, boas don't mind. In fact, once-a-week feeding is just about right.

Boas have more good points. They don't require much space, and they're odorless. Better yet, they don't carry diseases that affect humans. Given proper care, they're clean, healthy animals.

Handling a boa

A small, well-fed boa will never attack a human. Neither will it bite unless someone handles it roughly. A curious child who forces a boa's mouth open, for example, is asking for trouble. As with any animal bite, the wound should be treated properly. There is always danger of infection.

When well cared for, boas tame easily. They cannot be taught to sit up or roll over, but they will learn to trust the person who handles them. After a week or two, they'll coil around the handler's body and can be carried almost anywhere.

Very few people turn their boas loose in the house. There's always a chance that they'll escape. That means the owners must buy mice or rats at a pet store to feed their boas. Seldom are friends invited in to watch the boa feed. Unless the guests understand snakes, they'll feel sorry for the mice.

What do the experts say?

Should you buy a boa? Wildlife experts hope everyone will think twice before doing so. They believe

The boa constrictor is an important link in the balance of nature.

that all wild animals belong in their natural habitats. After all, living in a box isn't anything like life in the jungle. In addition, the experts worry that taking boas and other wild animals from their habitat will upset the balance of nature.

MAP:

Most boa constrictors in North and South America are found within the shaded areas.

46

INDEX/GLOSSARY:

BINOCULAR VISION 17 — Having two eyes arranged so as to see objects in 3-D (three dimensions).

BURROW 8, 13, 21, 22 — A hole or tunnel in the ground that an animal uses for shelter.

COLD-BLOODED 8, 21 — Having lack of control over body temperature.

GESTATION 29 — The time it takes for young animals to develop within the female's body.

HABITAT 13, 20, 21, 28, 40, 45 — The place where an animal makes it home.

HERPETOLOGIST 9, 19, 27, 28, 36 — A scientist who studies snakes and other reptiles.

JACOBSON'S ORGAN 18, 33 — A special organ in the roof of a snake's mouth that "taste-smells" material picked up by the tongue.

INSTINCTS 34 — Natural behaviors that are inborn in an animal.

KERATIN 14 — The hard material from which a snake's scales are formed.

MOLTING 16, 32, 33 — The process by which a snake sheds its old, worn-out skin.

MYTH 35, 36, 37 — Belief or story that is accepted unquestioningly.

PARASITES 27, 28, 33 — Any insect, worm, or germ that lives on, or in, an animal and feeds on the animal's body.

PREY 13, 18, 19, 22, 23, 27, 31, 33, 39 — Animals hunted for food by other animals.

SCALES 8, 16, 20, 27, 33 — Tough, protected plates that are part of a boa constrictor's skin.

VERTEBRAE 19 — The chain of bones that make up the flexible backbone of a snake.

47

WILDLIFE
HABITS & HABITAT

READ AND ENJOY THE SERIES:

If you would like to know more about all kinds of wildlife, you should take a look at the other books in this series.

You'll find books on bald eagles and other birds. Books on alligators and other reptiles. There are books about deer and other big-game animals. And there are books about sharks and other creatures that live in the ocean.

In all of the books you will learn that life in the wild is not easy. But you will also learn what people can do to help wildlife survive. So read on!